Matthew 6:25–34
for children

Jesus Teaches Us Not to Worry

Written by Julie Stiegemeyer

Illustrated by Larry Johnson

CONCORDIA PUBLISHING HOUSE · SAINT LOUIS

On a grassy hillside,
    in the shining sun,
people came together,
    gathering as one.

The crowds came there to listen,
    stretched out on the ground,
fathers, mothers, daughters, sons,
    were sitting all around.

There they heard a single voice,
  a message filled with grace,
of hope and promise from the Lord:
  God's love in Jesus' face.

No, the birds aren't anxious;
    they don't lose any sleep.
They simply close their eyes in peace
    and rest when night is deep.

Their loving heavenly Father
    gives them rich supply.
He blesses them with food and drink;
    their needs He'll satisfy.

And God cares for His children,
    just like each little bird.
He gives us everything we need;
    we trust His Holy Word.

Then Jesus told the people
      to look out on the field
to see how God's rich blessings
      there a harvest yield.

The lilies bloom in splendor;
      God clothes them in His care.
They do not spin or labor;
      God gives them what they wear.

If flowers trust the Father
      will give them everything,
so we, the Father's children,
      should also trust our King.

God's highest, most-loved creatures,
    His daughters and His sons,
are clothed and fed and nourished;
    we're God's most cherished ones.

Yes, our Father clothes us
    and gives us daily food.
He gives us homes and families;
    all things are for our good.

But even more, He grants to us
    eternal life as well.
Because of Jesus' death for us,
    with God we'll ever dwell.

Those times when you have troubles
or worries large or small,
God knows before you have them
and cares about them all.

He knows when you are bullied.
    He knows when you are stressed.
He knows when you are feeling sick,
    or when you fail a test.

So listen to the Savior
    and trust His loving Word.
Remember how His love extends
    to every flower and bird.

And so much more He cares for you,
    in each and every way.
So do not doubt His tender care,
    but rest in it today.

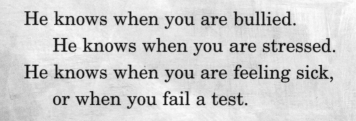

Dear Parents,

This portion from Matthew 6 is part of a larger section of Scripture commonly referred to as Jesus' Sermon on the Mount. In the surrounding chapters (Matthew 5–7), Jesus teaches the Lord's Prayer and shares the "Beatitudes" or the "Blesseds," those well-known sayings of His that begin, "Blessed are the . . ."

The basis of this book is a relatively brief section of Matthew 6 that focuses on God's gracious provisions to us. He says, rather poignantly, how trusting the birds and flowers are. We feel the weight of His words as we realize just how much we have, how much God gives, and how much we worry. Yet, even though we may feel our lack of faith, God continues to graciously love us and reassure us that He is trustworthy and true. His love is not dependent on us. He gives freely, just because it's who He is.

As you read and discuss this book with your children, ask what may be weighing on their minds. What may seem trivial or childish to an adult can be of real concern to children, who may indeed feel anxious about such things. Most adults know that stomach-churning feeling of nagging worry and concern; children may experience that as well.

Reassuring your children that God will continue to provide and care for them through all circumstances will help to nurture their faith in Christ and in His gracious love. We can tell children that through God's gracious provisions for us, He not only gives us all of the material blessings we need to support our body and life but He also gives us much more. God grants us eternal life through the loving gift of Jesus' death on the cross. After all, our God, "who did not spare His own Son but gave Him up for us all, how will He not also with Him graciously give us all things?" (Romans 8:32).

The author

What did Jesus tell the crowds?
　What did Jesus say?
He told them of God's tender care;
　He taught them how to pray.

Just as Moses, long before,
　went up on a hill,
Jesus now taught all who heard:
　He would God's Word fulfill.

Lord Jesus told the people
　of God's unending love,
how everything they needed
　came from God above.

"Do not worry," Jesus said,
  "about what you will eat.
God will give you all you need—
  water, bread, and meat.

"See the birds up in the air;
  they neither sow nor reap.
They do not store their goods in barns;
  they do not extras keep.

"Imagine how a bird might be
  fretting in his nest;
troubled by his problems,
  he'd never get to rest."